The Omitted Tribe Stories: Sheol

Brooks Crittenton

Royal Media and Publishing
Jeffersonville, IN
http://royamediaandpublishing.com
royalmediapublishing@gmail.com

© Copyright – 2024

All Rights Reserved. No part of this book may be reproduced, stored in a retrieval system, or transmitted by any means without the written permission of the author.

Cover Design: Gad Elite Book Covers

ISBN-13: 978-1-955501-20-0

Printed in the United States of America

Dedication

I dedicate this book to The Most-High for blessing me with a gift.

My wife for supporting me and being by my side.

Grandma Crittenton and Grandma Orndorff, thank you.

Family, friends, and fans thanks for the support and pushing me to be better.

Mrs. Julia thank you for giving the opportunity of changing a hobby to a career.

Sheol Outline

<u>Judeawai</u> is the beautiful city which has been practicing centuries worth of peace

Characters of Sheol
- Poe- Peace on Earth-The chosen new king
- Nia- Poe's Mother
- Elijah- Poe's friend
- Aminah- Poe's Girlfriend-the chosen new queen, an angelic being
- Yah/Adir- The heavenly father who looks out for all his children
- Erykah- Aminah's Mom
- Aminah's Grandmother-instilled the value of prayer
- Aminah's Great-grandmother- She stitched up the wedding dress, Aminah's father's grandmother, such angelic being
- Rose- Aminah's friend, who is committed to duty
- The old Man- Crazy old man in Judeawai
- Orion- Party Thrower
- Luna- twin younger sister to Muna, who is attuned to the moon
- Muna- The older twin to Luna
- King Jodi- Leader of Judeawai, first king of non-royal blood

- Queen Kathleen-she protects her king from any danger, compared to nature
- Azel- he was supposed to be the next heir, he is of royal blood, the son of a savage
- Mycki- The right hand to Jodi. His protector and guide.
- Tribal Society- The members who make decisions with the King to make Judeawai better. There are 12 members including the King
- Jodi's Mother- She prayed her non-royal son will be king
- Ravana- A general in the making
- Tris- The event lady.
- Aiyden- Orion's friend, an accomplice of disrupting the Peace
- King Denali- The last royal king of Judeawai
- Mother Kawana- Mother of the village, who watches all the children
- Slave Owner- Owns Elijah for his crimes
- The Shadows- an elite organization, there purpose disrupt centuries of Peace
- Axel- Father of Azel, a proud man with royal blood, his family was promised to be next in line
- Alo- The right-hand guide to King Denali
- The Lady in the Shadows- Made such plans to disrupt the ceremony.

Table of Contents

Dedication	iii
Sheol Outline	v
21 Years Earlier	1
1. The Beginning	3
2. The Lotus	10
3. Last Night	16
4. Tribal Society	22
5. The Celebration	30
6. A Forbidden Love	39
7. The Ceremony Bells	51
8. A Forgotten Dream	69
9. A Dream Come True	81
10. A Failed Challenge	107
Author Note	127
Epilogue	129
Other Books by This Author	134

21 Years Earlier

The moon was dripping blood.
It was the night my parents fell in love.
Seeing a being I have never seen above,
Hitting my head on my wall, screaming.
Why Am I Not Enough?
You had me, why are you not happy?
All I hear is peace; a whole community can't recognize me.
Mother. I was born from your womb; Father, I was a present given to Mom in your room.
I came to exist from the inexperience of y'all's love.
My head is leaking, moon lend me some blood.
Parents, my only question is
Why Am I Not Enough?
The rain is pouring outside.
Above, is a different type of light.
My father was yelling at my mother about a newborn daughter.
Looking at the clouds in the sky, asking them why,
I see glee in my father's eyes.
Lightning reaching, thunder chasing,
I heard the sound of the blood hitting dirt,
Making mud on the ground.
Why do my tears hurt?

Why is no one coming for me now?
In all this commotion, how did I hear the tear of my father's shirt?
My father's voice seems to be getting farther now.
I'm uncomfortable with this silence now.
There are two ladies sitting down.
"Girl, this baby will make you so proud,
with your husband, love you can finally allow."
"Nia, shh, such things you shouldn't say aloud,
the oldest is upstairs," my mother said.
With blood in her hand, she screams, "Nia!"
With this blood of the moon, I will make.
This Vow
On this day, I vow to change a society.
On this day, I vow to have hatred toward that li'l lady.
On this day, I vowed in the shadows.
On this day, I will embrace
This Vow.

1. The Beginning

I dwell in a rich and beautiful city.
Dawn's hue is always soothing.
The peoples' bronze skin glow is unforgetting.
Busy talking, fast walking, doesn't happen often.
We are a peaceful folk.
Words carefully thought out when spoke.
I hear it, it's getting louder; my city just awoke.
Celebration beginning, my head is spinning.
Why were my dreams provoked?
My phone starts ringing, my mind still thinking.
Answering this phone, with a tone
That I want to be left alone.
"Hello."
"Poe, you just waking up?" said Elijah.
"Yeah."
"Well, get your ass up. We are about to slide on ya."
"Ight, but give me a minute."
Wiping my eyes, getting out of bed, smelling food,
I made my way to the kitchen,
To see what my mother was fixing.

My Mother

An angel sent down from heaven by Yah.
An example of what it looks like to beat all odds.
Beautiful, quiet, and smart,
Her actions are led by her heart.

Every day, she teaches about love.
Says even when you're lost,
Listen to the words of the one above.
Strong, brilliant, and protective,
It's been like this for all my years.
She fights my fears and wipe my tears.
I will always love her because she is.

<u>My Mother</u>

"Poe!"
"Yes, ma'am?"
"Fix your plate and start eating. I have to get ready for the celebration."
I grabbed my plate, filling it with eggs, pancakes and bacon.
My favorite meal of the day is breakfast.
Sitting down, staring at this food,
Wondering why my dream has left me so restless,
Not noticing my mom was studying me.
"Baby, you alright? I heard you tossing and turning all night."
"I'm all right, I guess it was this dream I had."
"Well, tell me about your dream."
"Oh, so now you Joseph, you can tell me what dreams mean. With that bright color nightgown you're wearing?"
My mother made a smirk but never stopped staring.

"Boy, tell me your dream."
"We were at the celebration, everybody was having a great time. The ol' folk were sipping on wine or whatever. Kids trying to sneak a drink, the ol' folk screaming out, "Y'all know better," the kids start running and the old ones started reminiscing about their younger days. Music playing, people dancing, young couples are romancing. Just when everybody is at the peak of having fun, the clouds turn black, the sky turns bright red. From the sky, are falling balls of fire, like that young couple's desire. The squeals get higher every time the ground meets fire. People are burning, my stomach is turning. Then I heard a loud voice in the skies, saying, "This is because of your eyes.""
"Or it was saying, lies?"
"Honestly, I don't know. It felt so real."
"Calm down and eat your meal. Everything is going to be okay, Peace. Oh, did I do that, wasn't I the one who picked your name? Do you know what I love to hear?
"No, ma'am."
"Your name. Okay, in a strong voice, say your name."
"Peace on Earth!" said Poe.
"That's right, the whole ride to the hospital, I kept saying it's going to be all right, Poe. When you

were born, the doctors wanted a full name so I said, "Peace On Earth, my little Poe." So you feeling down? What did I used to tell you when you were upset? And you'd better not act like you don't know.

POE
Out of me, came Poe,
A little Peace On Earth.
Every day, I will guide you and show your worth.
One day, you'll be able to heal the hurt.
You are my Peace On Earth.
If you ever get misguided,
Say your name loud and be reminded,
You are my Peace On Earth.
May not understand now,
But in a while,
The stars will twinkle and the sun will smile.
Their light will guide you for miles.
The world will know,
Out of me came Poe,
A little Peace On Earth.

POE
"Thanks, Mom, for always being there."
"No problem, but you'd better go upstairs, your phone is ringing. I guess it's time for you to get ready."
Running, skipping steps,

Thinking to myself, *I ain't even pick out my clothes yet.*

Negative energy, I must reject.

Getting ready for this Celebration, I must respect.

My chucks are fresh.

I'm dressed to impress.

Elijah at the door, we ready to step.

Elijah

The homie for real.

He's wise and dangerous, someone ready to kill.

Homies for years,

One of the few who has seen my tears.

He's more than flesh.

His spirit demands respect.

While being on this earth,

It was told, in his own way, he will show your worth.

Elijah

"Bruh, you ready?" asked Elijah.

"Man, you know I stay ready," said Poe.

"Is that Elijah at the door?"

"Yes, ma'am," said Poe.

"How are you doing, Mrs. Nia?"

"Elijah, I'm doing well, not much to tell.

But y'all be safe and have fun today."

Both said, "Yes, ma'am,"

And they walked out the door.

Fun is what they wanted to get into, for sure.
Palm tree leaves swaying in the breeze,
The sunlight giving proper energy to my city,
It's safe, it's beautiful, it's gritty.
It's powerful, its knowledge, it's busy.
It's risky, it's silly, it's witty.
Celebrating a few hundred years of peace.
The elders try to explain how it used to be.
Something you wouldn't want to see.
We heard things you wouldn't want to believe.
It was hectic, it was biblical and poetic,
The wrong to ourselves was in our genetics.
Our city comes together every year so we don't forget it.
Elijah starts to pour juice to make us more energetic.
Poe rolls the herb to help the kinetic.
Smiles on many peoples' faces,
Children running fast, chasing,
Each other, dreams, whatever.
Not concerned about consequences that will eventually make them better,
Elijah and Poe passing the earth amongst each other.
Elijah said, "My bad for not making it out last night."

Poe replied, "Bruh, it's all good, the turnout was ight.

2. The Lotus

Those eyes opened,
When she heard the noise.
The boys and girls joking,
With their loud outside voices.
Wiping away the sleep,
Still trying to decipher her dream,
It was startling how could she not know what it means.
Fire falling from the skies.
Hearing little children cry.
Grabbing her favorite brush,
Stroking her hair.
Looking through her grandmother's mirror,
Listening for a voice that's not clear.

Aminah
You're beautiful and clever.
You're irresistible and a treasure.
Out of the womb, you made your parents better.
Such a marvel and wonder to see.
You were blessed from head to feet.
Your spirit is solid and your energy is free.
It's been proclaimed that one day you will be queen.
Just know if anyone crosses you,
That's somebody I wouldn't want to be.

Aminah

As she was finishing her hair,
Her mother was calling her from downstairs.
"Girl, are you up yet? I got the table set,
With fresh squeezed orange juice in your cup," her mother said.
Looking one more time in the mirror,
Her grandmother's voice was clearer.
"Baby, whenever you feel troubled,
Never forget your prayer."

The Forgotten Prayer

Adir, I am lost and need you here.
My soul is cold, your warmth I need near.
Mine eyes don't work, so
Please lend me divine sight, to see clear.
Open my earthly ears,
For me to properly hear.
Adir, I am lost and need you here.

The Forgotten Prayer

In an instant, all worry was gone.
Time to run down the stairs.
Right past her mother, she sat in her favorite chair.
Her mother,
So petite and mean,
Such a beauty you've never seen.
A true definition of love that only few have seen.
"Mom," said Aminah.
"Yes, dear?" replied her mother.

I woke up to my spirit troubled
Like never before.
Gazing through grandma's mirror,
I ended up reciting The Forgotten Prayer.
And just in a blink of an eye, I felt better.
It was weird; I had no fear."
Her mother, in a soft tone, said, "Come here."
Aminah walked over there,
Smelling her perfume,
A scent that can swallow a room.

Erykah

A woman of wisdom,
An example of spiritual freedom,
She reaches impossible heights.
A daughter, a mother, an amazing wife,
Her heart shines a different light.
Never shied away from a fight,
This woman was a different type.

Erykah

"Baby, do you know why your grandmother called it The Forgotten Prayer?"
"No."
"It's because our city doesn't pray anymore,
Even though we celebrate every year.
We honestly, as a whole, forget what we do this for.
As a family, we should be thankful for our lineage,

The ancient prayers is our heritage.
Or, maybe you're afraid,
Because this is a life-changing day?
Have you talked to that boy, anyway?"
"No, ma'am. Actually, I haven't spoken to him in a couple days."
"You got yourself a fine man, you should be excited," said Erykah.
"So why do I feel so exhausted? Just recently, I feel we lost our connection," said Aminah.
"Baby, in the art of romancing, there are always chances."
Just remember…

The Lotus
In the mud, there was a couple who was hopeless.
Through them, was born a lotus.
What a beauty, something to notice.
Her parents was focused.
They knew their purpose was to make this child feel special.
Polish the petals, stray away from any pedestals,
Intentionally teaching to always be expressible
And if they walk this path,
Their life will be hysterical.

The Lotus
Please, I need for you to get ready.
Because your family is on the way.

After eating all her food,
Aminah went to her room, feeling in a good mood.
As she opened her closet,
She marveled at her dress,
The same one her great-grandmother stitched to impress. To have a such a possession,
How lucky, how blessed.
Throughout her whole family,
She was in line, she was next.
As she was thinking,
Her phone started ringing.
"Hello."
"Girl, why didn't you step out last night?" asked Rose.
"I wasn't feeling it. I guess I needed some rest," Aminah said.
"Today's your day, though… how are you feeling?"
"I'm dealing."
"I don't know why you're tripping, you 'bout to throw on that bad dress and step to live your best."
"I guess, if my girl says so."
"I say so; call me when you're on the way."
"Okay," said Aminah.
"We have been friends for a long time and I'm happy you found love, though.
So I ask, how do you know you love him?

I'm asking for me."
"Girl, I love him from the crown on his head,
To the wiggly toes on his feet."
"Are you sure this is unconditional, for an eternity?"
"Rose, he's here for me," Aminah said.
They spoke a little longer, but Aminah had to hang up the phone to get ready.

3. Last Night

"I heard last night was wild. I woke up thinking I should've just gone out. Bruh, you'd better tell me what went down last night," said Elijah.

"Aight," said Poe.

Aiyden hit my line and said Orion was throwing a party.

Elijah said, "I never really liked those two, they the type to scheme and set you up."

I headed out,

The moment I get there, drinks in cups.

Everybody wilding, bruh, you know the twins Luna and Muna.

"Yeah, but I don't like them."

"They was on some type of drug, in the living room, giving Orion bedroom type of love. The women were wearing lingerie with a mask as if they were throwing a masquerade. This party had women for days. You know my situation, so I didn't know if I should leave or stay, but the music was playing, the people were dancing, some folk at the table laying spades. I'm already on my drink, you know I'm straight. A couple of hours go by, don't know how many shots I took to the face. The energy was strong, I couldn't get away.

Out of nowhere, this mysterious lady started to lure me into this space."

Elijah said, "What about—"

"For a split second, I saw her face, closed my eyes and felt the woman's hands on my waist. Time, she didn't want to waste."

My Mistake

"I apologize, I'm weak to pleasure.
These lines crossed can break a union forever.
I started thinking I needed to get out altogether,
But her warm hands made me feel better.
No time to think consequences.
Go left, go right, why she had to be so submissive?
Finger over my lips, she wanted this private.
In the silence, we were breathing as one.
After this short alliance, she had me feeling dumb.
She got up, smiling.
I was wondering, *what have I done?*"

My Mistake

Elijah said, "How can you let that be?"

"Man, all I know, she was gripping at my every need. For a moment, I felt free, but I got a feeling she knew me. It was deceiving," said Poe.

"What are you going to do?" asked Elijah.

"Realize I made a mistake and keep moving," replied Poe.

Taking a sip out of his cup, watching the children run by, the smoke between his fingers was rising in the sky.

Elijah said, "Bruh, it's all good. You not the first and won't be the last. Long as last night you had a blast, memories you will always have."
"I know what you mean, but when I went home and went to sleep, I had a horrible dream," said Poe.
Elijah said, "It sounds like you need more herb to me."
An old man walking by, says,
"Someone will bring destruction from the skies, we will hear, on the lies, a King will come in due time, when the crown is placed, evil will show his face."
Poe's nightmare started playing in his mind,
This old man had to be out his mind.
Peace is what Poe is trying to find.
Orion pulled up at this time.

Orion

Someone who don't care about nothing.
Only if it's about something.
And that's on anything.
He the type to get it by any means.
Be cautious cuz he can snatch many dreams.

Orion

"What up, Poe?" said Orion.
"Last night, I heard you got lit,
Heard you got into some shit."

Elijah thought how he knew this but didn't say anything.
Poe said, "What do you mean?"
"Sounded like you had a great time to me.
Ain't you? Aren't you, chosen for the celebration?"
Poe said, "Yeah."
"That's so amazing,"
Said Orion before pulling off.
"Bruh, I never trusted that dude.
Aiyden always seemed koo,
But when those two get together,
No telling what they will do," said Elijah.

***

Luna
A sister of two, a twin,
A twisted kind of friend.
One who's attuned with the moon.
Been in the trenches,
With the coldest of goons.
Luna
She'd seen him come in,
After she was done with him,
her mask on, walking in the back.
"He's here, the time is near," Luna said.
 A silhouette of a figure,

Breaking down what looked like pills.
Just in this presence, will make your soul chill.
This body can be compared to no other.
Pouring the powder in a cup with the liquor,
Mixing it.
"He's here?"
Luna said, "Yes."
"Give him this and watch how the story begins."
As Luna walked out the room,
She saw the evil smile on the mysterious face.
Luna moved her feet swiftly, so the plan could be in place,
Handing the cup to her sister.

Muna

Beautiful, easy on the eyes,
She has hate, she has might.
She has will, she has sight.
The oldest of two, a twin.
Vindictive wishes,
Sleep with the dead to get riches.

Muna

Luna said, "Not a drop, you'd better waste, a second one is being prepared for the chase."
"Little sister, I move with style and grace,
Your older sister never makes mistakes," replied Muna.
With her mask on,

She walked out the room,
Then got lost in the sea of women
In the hallway.
Every girl had the same mask on her face.
It was a masquerade.
It was a party with drinks.
Luna sipped her champagne,
Excited for a change.
300 years of peace,
She wanted to see hurt and pain.
No sunlight, she needed the moon,
To raise the grave.
The Beginning Song
The words will be sung,
By a beauty so young.
From not knowing what she wants,
A new beginning will begin.
We will connect with our kin,
From deep within.
The Beginning Song

4. Tribal Society

Pouring the drink in his cup,
Looking over the things he must discuss
With the council.
Eleven different faces,
Eleven different minds.
Grateful he gets to see a celebration
Another time.
He opened the envelope and saw
Poe and Aminah.
I remember them when they were children.
Thinking on this,
While his drink, he was sipping.

Jodi

What a leader, what a man.
He's proved since birth he can.
What a speaker, he never ran.
The ones before him knew his worth.
He is the plan.

Jodi

His phone rings. "Hello."
"Excuse me, sir, it's about five minutes before the meeting."
"Thank you." The caller hangs up.
Finishing his drink, Jodi places down his cup.
This year, he knew it was going to be rough.
Since the elders were teaching,

He was designed to be tough.
Because he was not of royal blood.
His phone rings again. "Hello."
"Your first council is about to begin."

His Wife

So lit, such candor,
This queen will never quit, slow to anger.
A special type of spirit.
Protects her husband from danger,
Kathleen is compared to nature.

His Wife

"Yes, ma'am," said Jodi.
"You will be straight, you, my king, you great."
"Thank you, queen. You remember Poe and Aminah? They were chosen for the ceremony this year. Poe is going to be something special, you'll see."
"I grew up with Aminah's mother; her father was an elder. You're ready for your meeting, did you sip on your favorite beverage?"
"I'm ready and why do you act like you know me?"
"Because I do know you. Well, do your thing, king," said Kathleen.
"Love you."
"Love you too." Then they hung up
Scanning the room, to make sure he grabbed everything before he left the room.

***

Their voices were in the back room.
Over the new extended, king-sized table, they loomed.
Discussing the old traditions they only knew.
Azel spoke in a vile tone,
When new traditions were spoken.

Azel

Next in line, he was the heir.
The only of few, you can feel his glare,
Throughout the air.
He is vile, who will dare?
His father is Axel, he is the son of a savage.
He'll never forget,
That he came up short on that challenge.
This baggage, he can't balance.

Azel

"Y'all first know I should've been chosen,
These new traditions are hopeless."
His words echoed down the hallways.
Azel had no fear in his voice.
It was his choice, it was clear.
He didn't care about any repercussion on
What he'd just said.

"It seems, this morning, Azel has a lot on his head."
Azel spun around,
Looking at King Jodi with his red eyes.
Jodi stared through his eyes,
As he walked by.
"Good morning, everybody," said the king.
"Morning, King," the response of nine
Members sitting down in their chairs.
The king noticed Azel still standing there.

Jodi and Azel
This whole journey, has been their life.
Jodi was accomplished, Azel always failed.
With the elders, Jodi was honored.
Azel was loved by his father.
Any task, compared to Azel, he slaughtered.
This upset his forefathers.
For this reason, it pushed Jodi harder.
'Neath his red eyes, was forming a warmonger.

Jodi and Azel
"Are you going to sit in your chair?"
Azel knew he didn't want to challenge here.
He looked at the nine faces before he sat in his chair.
In the room, the tension was clear.
Something was lurking and rising.
Then the doors opened surprisingly.

"Azel, out of everyone, don't you practice traditions? Even if the laws change, we still honor our heritage. We always give respect to who our king is," said Mycki.

Mycki
The right hand to Jodi,
Inclined spiritually.
Passed down from fathers,
Generations begotten.
Making sure "we know who we are."
Is not forgotten.

Mycki
The other elders following behind,
An interesting group, never knowing what was on anyone's mind, their seats, they try to find.
While whispering low,
The eyes are on King Jodi,
They're ready for him to go.
The king begins to speak.
"I can't believe he's king, the first time in history, where it's not in their veins,"
Said Azel.
"Yeah, when the elders announced Jodi,
I thought it was strange, but it was always predicted it would be Jodi the No Name," said Ravana.
"And as his right, he called Mycki,"

Snarled Azel.
"Now that I've got everybody's attention,
It's time to speak on the celebration.
The union we have for the ceremony,
Is Poe and Aminah.
Azel stood out of his chair.
He didn't care. "This is disgusting, exactly what I was discussing. Does royal blood even matter anymore?"
Mycki let out a low roar, "Azel, your comment to the king was uncalled for."
Jodi raised his hand, saying,
"Let me make this as clear as I can,
In front of everyone.
Azel, the reason you are mad, I understand.
The reason why you are not up here, is because you can't. Don't you think we disrespect the royal blood? Since you are about tradition, Mycki, hand me my weapon.
Which route do you want to go, Azel? You're the only one who can answer that question."
Jodi's muscles started flexing.
Azel, analyzing the situation,
Realized to sit down.
Jodi said, "It won't be easy to take this crown. If you didn't know, we are moving in times,
And I've thought about this. Poe is next in line."

Those words did something to Azel's mind.
Azel spoke. "Where is the blood line?"
The king looked at Azel and said, "Aminah."
"Mixing royal blood."
"Is the direction for this ceremony. This couple is in love," said the king.
Do you know what this celebration means?
The Meaning
This is thanks to our peace,
Where unions come together,
Because 300 years ago, we were not free.
Able to be, we,
The melanated people,
Who see no equal.
We are here to give thanks for our peace.
The Meaning
"The people will know we're here for their needs," said the king.
"Are we done here? I don't think I need a history lesson. But, oh, King, can I leave, with your blessing?"
The king nodded his head.
Looking to the rest, he continued to move ahead.
You Will See
Tribal Society, one day, you will see.
I will stand in front of you as king,
Run these lands, as it should be.

Oh, my Tribal Society, one day, you will see.
I will sit in front of you as king,
Getting pleased by my queen.
Oh, my Tribal Society, one day, you will see.
You Will See

5. The Celebration

So many people are outside,
The skies are nice, the birds are out to fly.
"For real, bruh, are you alright?"
"Yeah, just startled by last night," said Poe.
The music is playing, people are dancing.
I always loved this time of year,
Every generation laughing with cheer.
Grateful they're here.
Chanting the

Sing Along

Sing along,
If you know this song.
Right hand up, if you know you're strong.
Left hand up, if you have a home.
If you don't,
Then you're not alone.
We will bless,
With what He has shown.

Sing Along

"Hey, bruh, sing along if you know the song," Elijah said.
"That song is annoying. They sing the song all day," said Poe,
Walking through the crowd,
Trying to make their way.

"Being chosen, does that make your mom proud?" asked Elijah.
"Actually, she hasn't really even spoken.
I think it's still a shock that I was chosen.
She likes Aminah,
But lately, my mother's been a little off.
I can't put my finger on it," said Poe.
"That's a lot, low key special, because it gives hope to those who don't have royal blood.
The city is changing."
"And I think that's what's making my mother anxious. It's like she feels something but won't say anything," said Poe.
The music is getting louder.
It's finally approaching the hour…
***
It's noisy.
Her ears are hurting.
She can tell her heart is working, it's pumping.
This is a day she's always been wanting.
The dancers are jumping,
Her phone starts buzzing.
"Hello."
"Girl, are you coming?" asked
Rose
A friend of beauty,
Thorns rarely to be seen.

She's there in the morning and in death.
A friend of beauty,
Maybe one day, she should be queen.
She's there when he wants it and
The king will have no breath.
A friend of beauty,
Who is committed to duty.

Rose

"Yes, I'm on the way," said Aminah.
"Didn't I say call me when you were on the way?" said Rose.
"Well, I knew you would call anyway."
"I'm so excited, ready to see you in that beautiful dress that's stitched to impress," replied Rose.
"Like I said, I'm on the way. I'll call you when I get there, promise," Aminah said
As she was hanging up the phone.
"Aminah, are you okay? And you'd better be honest," asked her mother.
With tears in her eyes, Aminah cried,
"I haven't seen him. I'm anxious. After today, what will it be like? Mom, the responsibility of being chosen, it's too much pressure. I don't think I can do it anymore."
"Miss lady, I need you to be aware, anything in this world, you can bear," Erykah said.

"Baby, you need to know your lineage, what makes our family such savages…

Just then, Aminah's mind drifts.

Aminah's Prayer

Adir, your child is lost and I need you here.
Erase this cold, your warmth I need near.
These humanly possessions don't work so,
Please lend me divine sight, to see clear.
Open these earthly ears,
For me to properly hear.
Adir, your child Aminah is lost,
And I need you here.

Aminah's Prayer

"I'm telling you, your great-grandmother is the reason the family is so savagely beautiful. Never giving her right to a high place when her husband died. Your great-grandmother made your great-grandfather cry at the wedding. The story has it, that moment was very unforgettable. They say before that day, that man couldn't cry."

"Why, I mean how?" replied Aminah.

The Dress

Your great-grandfather didn't have any money, yet alone for a dress.
He worked till his back hurt,
that was just the wedding cost.

Your great-grandmother wanted a dress that was for the well-off.
Every night, he tried.
Every night, she stitched.
Anything for his future bride.
Anything for the man who asked to hitch.
When she walked down that aisle, he cried.
Because he saw the dress your great-grandmother stitched.

The Dress

Explained her mother, "Aminah, I need you to know who you are.
Baby, you are the twinkle in the stars.
The universe resides in who you are."
Aminah looked at the crowd.
She said, "Mother, I know this now, it's just I don't know what to do now."
Looking again, she saw Mrs. Nia in the crowd.
"Mom, hold up, I gotta see her smile," said Aminah.

***

"This celebration, why my son, my love?
What are these elders up to,
He has no royal blood?"
"Mrs. Nia." Her name, she thought she heard.

Looking around, she didn't see anyone she'd recognize.
As she was walking, she ran into a girl holding a dress, stitched to impress.
Looking into those innocent eyes,
"Aminah," said Nia.
"Yes, I'm on my way to the ceremony,
And I'm really worried. Wait, where are you going?" asked Aminah.
Getting last minute items for this special day."
"It's good to see you," said Aminah.
"Look at this dress, my son will be impressed.
The stars aligned when he was born,
So he'll be blessed. Since being with you,
He doesn't seem as stressed.
Aminah, after this ceremony, you will be family," said Nia.
"I appreciate your love, what would you want from me?" Aminah asked.

My Baby

"Aminah, please, all I ask is look after my baby.
Sometimes his actions may make you crazy.
All I ask is look after my baby.
Please watch over Peace, my little baby.
I will always respect the lady,
Who protects my baby."

My Baby

"My son is a lot of joy and really loves you," said Nia.

"Got me having these tears in my eyes, I really appreciate your time. Make sure you're there When I'm walking down that aisle.

I have to see your smile," said Aminah.

"All right, go on; it's close to that time. I know your mom is going out of her mind."

"Yeah, kinda, but she's fine," said Aminah.

"Like I said, you're beautiful, no need to worry. I'm happy you're becoming a part of our family," said Mrs. Nia.

Aminah, holding that dress to impress, got swallowed in the crowd. Nia's spirit was uneasy. Why was she more anxious now? She decided, before the ceremony, she had to sit Poe down. Just then, she heard the wind whisper, "Nia."

That voice was familiar, yet a stranger.

Looking down the dark hallway,

"Nia!"

The hairs on her back stood up.

Something let her know, this voice was dangerous…

***

"Are we going to still kick it when your chosen training begins?" asked Elijah.
"Bruh, not much will change.
Every day, we'll roll the herb.
It's all the same," said Poe.
"Have you been feeling different since the news?"
"All I've been doing is reflecting on self,
Because I don't know why they didn't ask someone else. Being chosen, was that ever a dream when you were a youngin'?" asked Poe.

A Dream
When I was a little boy,
I dreamed of hearing a lot of noise.
From the city, knowing,
Even when I was hopeless,
That I was the chosen.
Proud of who I am,
A everyday resident with no royal in his veins,
I will conquer all.
No longer would people look at me the same.
When I was a little boy
I dreamed of hearing a lot of noise.

A Dream
"Yeah, that was a younger dream, a younger me, but you got me able to believe
If we work hard, anything, we can achieve."

"I feel ya, low key. Wonder what Aminah will wear," said Poe as he was sitting there.
"Poe, as we wait, let's put another one in the air.
This is a celebration all together.
A time to smoke amongst one another."
This year, the celebration was all the same.
The only thing different, the chosen name had changed,
And it was his name.

6. A Forbidden Love

There were different types of flower petals floating in the air,
A lot of people entering in here.
"King, I've never seen a ceremony quite like this," Mycki said.
"I know, not even for ours," said Kathleen.
This looks like it came straight out of someone's dream."
"King, this is one of the most beautiful things I've seen," said Mycki.
King Jodi was watching over all the people entering,
Understanding that he was making history.

His Mother

"Jodi, you will be something to see.
The day you came out of me,
I looked to the stars and asked for a king.
Something these people will need.
Our nation will see history.
A king from a low class lady.
If no one tells you that you're special."
At least he learned from

His Mother

"Your mother would be so proud today," said Kathleen.
As she set her eyes on her king…

***

The kids run by with their joyous screams,
Around Poe and Elijah, as they marveled at what they had just seen.
They both couldn't believe.
Poe thought, *Why for me?*
Outside, the dancers were shaking,
Making their way to that beautiful building.
The sun was gazing different.
The birds were acting distant.
They smelled fear.
I hear the banging in my ear.
This Celebration, This Ceremony…
"Poe, you need to go inside and get ready," said the lady running the event.
"Also, Elijah, there's something I need you to get."
She walked off to another conversation,
"All right, hey, bruh, check on my mom. I haven't seen her come in yet," said Poe.
"Once again, bruh, congratulations," said Elijah.
As he followed behind the lady,
Poe's heart was uneasy, and he started thinking,
I need my mom to pray for me.
He stepped into the magnificent building.
Once inside, everyone in there was busy,

Moving in every direction.
Worrying about the Ceremony, wanting this to be a great celebration.
Now, Poe wondered, *where's the room to get dressed?*
Time was getting close, was now the time to stress?
Which way to go, right or left?
Poe guessed left and stepped.

***

"Of course, bruh, I will look for your mom, no prob," said Elijah.
As he watched his homie walk off in the distance,
He saw Luna and Muna pointing and whispering.
"Man, what y'all laughing about on my homie's blessed day?"
They both looked at Elijah and laughed. "Yeah, it's going to be such a day."
As they both walked away,
Elijah sensed a different type of evil as they were bobbing through the people.
Someone snatched Elijah's wrist and said, "Follow me quickly…"

***

"Orion! Pay attention. So how did it go last night? Did everything go as planned?"
"Man, I threw the party of the century.
I had these two twins doing the nasty.
Every woman was in lingerie, I was throwing a masquerade."
"Orion! Boy, don't forget who you are talking to. Respect your place.
Now, answer my question. Did my plan get executed or not?"
Orion looked at the man towering over him.
"Yes, sir, the plan was executed," said Orion.

Don't Forget Why We Do This
Even in all your spotlight,
Don't forget why we do this.
Royal bloodline is pure, should not be mixed with their kind.
Don't forget why we do this,
Even if you have to take a life, to protect what's right.
Don't forget why we do this.
There will be no more light, we will survive in the dark.
Don't forget why we do this.

Don't Forget Why We Do This
"My whole life, I've seen peace, a city carefree.
I felt there was no reason for me to co-exist.

These chains of government are getting weak.
They will see; they will see.
Leave, go to the celebration."
Orion got up fast,
He had no time to be wasting.
"Nice little speech."
The man turned around and what he saw,

<u>In The Shadows</u>
In the shadows, she stays deep.
When she speaks, those chills creep.
Mysterious, she does seem.
In the shadows, she rests and sleeps.
She's safe and free.

<u>In The Shadows</u>
Just being in her presence, can make your soul chill.
"I told you this would unfold."
He asked, "How did you know?"
With a devilish smile, she replied, "I planted these seeds years ago."
After saying this, he followed her deeper into the shadows.

***

Why me? thought Aminah.
"Oh my goodness, doesn't she look so beautiful?"

"Yes, just like her older sister used to."
"Mama, remember you used to take me to this beautiful building when I was a child," said Aminah.
"Yes, I do, and look at you now. Today, this beautiful building and attention is on you," said Erykah.
"It's been a minute since I've seen a lot of my family.
They all are happy and proud, like me.
Most of all, excited to see what you will be."
The crowd was shouting.
The Ceremony would begin shortly.
Through the halls, it was heard, "The ceremony will begin shortly..."

***

"During the ceremony, No Named Jodi will be sitting there," said
__Ravana__
"A general in the making.
His family is the legion with many faces.
Don't get it mistaken, for many lives will be taken.
This monster, will do anything for the warmonger."
__Ravana__

"It's already there," said Azel.
Ravana, eyebrows raised,
"Do you think anyone will be aware?"
"No, 300 years of peace, the blood has remained royal
It's their fault, giving the average dreams of obtaining these titles."
"Oh, somebody in a mood today," said Ravana.
Those lips formed,
"Once the king gets handled the crown, will go to We."
Ravana asked, "So, I'll be standing here?" pointing at the chart.
"Yes."
"After you take care of the king, can I drive this knife through Poe's heart?
I just want to test the point," Ravana laughed.
As he said, "Get it, test the point," while touching the tip of his knife.
"Do what you must, but that child must die.
In front of everyone, looking them in the eyes.
Giving them a line, if they cross,
That's their life, their fault."
Getting up, laughing, they left the room.
Ravana shook his head and said,
"You were born for this."

Those eyes looked straight and those lips formed to say,

A Child
Out of a bunch, there would be this child.
Out of the bunch, this child would be wild.
Folk not knowing how to handle a child.
The one out of the bunch who was wild.

***

A Child
"Aminah, I need you to get ready," said the lady running the event.
She didn't realize, with her mom, how much time was spent.
Down the hallways, she went.
Some girls by her fast-skipped, with an unfamiliar type scent.
Under their breaths, they sang a song of resent.

This is Just A Song
"How much time do you think you get?
To betray your own, you won't forget.
This song is not a threat.
The pieces have just been set.
Please don't get upset, cuz.

This is Just A Song
For just a moment, Aminah felt fear.

Then, in her ears, she hears,
"The Ceremony will begin shortly."
Aminah started running, her blood pumping.
In the background, the drums are bumping.
Down the corner, she's turning, twisting handles.
One of these doors must open!
Before anybody sees her, she's hoping…

***

"Mycki, tell Tris, in 30 minutes, we should begin the event," said The king.
"But, sir, I am here to protect you. I don't like the way Azel has been moving lately," said Mycki.
"Ever since youth, we have been enemies. Not just us as beings. I mean, I represent the future. And he represents the past. This type of subject would make the elders clash," said Jodi.
Mycki looked at his king and said,
"You Are My King
It was you who made me see dreams,
Beyond any humanly thing.
We were nothing, now I ask, what's on your crown?
Who properly runs this town?
I am so proud,
You Are My King."

He left his king's side, looking for the main event lady.

***

This room Aminah was in, was big and dark.
There was something pulling at her heart.
Why did she feel so strange, knowing it was time to change?
Her clothes dropped to the floor. Aminah heard her name…

***

In this dark room, it was hard to change.
Pulling up his pants, just then he had to duck when he heard the door swing.
Who is coming in this room, what do I do? thought Poe.
As he was thinking, a girl start singing,
"All I Want is You
All I want is you.
Some folk won't think that I do.
All I know is you.
This belief holds me so true.
All I love is you.
You make me feel all brand new.

All I Want is You"

"Aminah!" Poe screamed.

***

Aminah turned around as if she was in a dream.
She thought, *oh, how he looks at me.*
Those thoughts started to get a little more crazy.
Her knees went weak when he told her
She was such a beautiful lady.
Now her body was going crazy.
"Poe, love me!"
Hearing those words, Poe held on to her curves.
She was his for sure.
This naked body was pure.

Forbidden Love

Hands have touched in different private places.
Different lips kissing on his face.
Intertwining in this embrace,
The heat is rising as they couldn't wait.
Love was being made, before the union can say,
"They do."
Kissing on necks, hair is being pulled.
Words were whispered, "This will always be yours."
Her reply was, "Are you sure?"
Before he went deeper, trying to love her more.

No bed, she was sprawled out on the floor, while receiving her
Forbidden Love

7. The Ceremony Bells

(14 Years Ago)

"People of the tribe of Judeawai, this will be the first ceremony. I want to do things in a different way," said King Denali.

"I would love to introduce Jodi and Kathleen; these two will be our future king and queen. This ceremony celebrates our peace and I want to show our unity in our community," said the king.

The people of the tribe screamed.

Jodi and Kathleen

Our future king and queen.

Royal blood and not, what will our generation see?

Jodi and Kathleen,

Have been chosen for royalty.

We are honored and we love

Jodi and Kathleen

"I can't believe the king would do such things."

Jodi and Kathleen stood facing the crowd.

Jodi noticed his mother in the front row, looking so proud.

"In seven years, these two will take the crown, chosen, they are now," Denali, the king, said.

As the dancers started dancing around,

They heard the drum beat, people moving their feet.

Moving and grooving around seats.

"Boy, look at me when I speak."
His son looked up and heard,
"You Disgust Me
Son, it was supposed to be you to lead.
You gave the crown to a common seed.
When you were born, I knew my son was the next heir to be.
Why have the angels punished me, by letting me birth something so weak?
Son, it was supposed to be you who leads.
But it was you who gave the crown to the common seed.
As your father, I need you to know,
You Disgust Me"
The son watched his dad turn his back and bump into people,
Until he no longer could see.
"One more time, let's give it up for this ceremony, celebrating our future king and queen."
The tribe gave one last scream for Jodi and Kathleen.
He was watching Jodi and Kathleen and couldn't believe that he couldn't wake from his dream as he heard those…

***

(Present Day)
Kathleen watched as Mycki left her husband's side.
She knew he was looking for the coordinator, so she would have a couple minutes outside.
The queen was pleased to look upon her tribe.
There was an old man who walked by, saying,
"Beware of the fire from the skies.
On this day, that flame will claim many lives."
One of the kids asked, "What did you say?"
The old man said, a little louder,
"Beware of the fire from the skies.
On this day, that flame will claim many lives."
The children chanted, rhythmically repeating, "The flame will claim many lives."
Following the old man in the distance.
In the queen's mind, there was a tatted image of

That Face
How I can ever forget
The worry, the hate?
He had brows of disgrace.
For destruction, she knew he'd wait.
Something inside warned she wouldn't forget.

That Face
The music was playing.
Dancers were moving, looking her way.
How this city danced to the beat.
It flowed through the queen's body.

She started to move her feet,
Skipping to the band's beat.
Looking up at a sky so blue,
How those words can't be true…

***

"Who is this, holding my wrist?"
Through the crowd, they were making turns and twists.
Down an alleyway, they went.
With force, the wall, his back hit.
"Who are you? What's the meaning of this?"
"Quiet!" said the mysterious person.
Elijah silently tried to collect his thoughts.
Who can this be?
Then he thought of Mrs. Nia.
"I don't know who you are, or what you are doing, but I got somewhere to be."
The mysterious person looked around, before dropping his mask to the ground.
"Aiyden?"
"Look, all I did was call Poe to the party.
I swear, I didn't know. Orion was going crazy."
"What do you mean?"
"I mean, I found out Orion linked himself with Some of the members of the society.

I promise, I only thought it was a party,
And I thought the ladies would get loose after they started drinking.
Orion, I started following, after his fun with the twins."
"Yeah, Poe told me about them."
"Orion was talking to this mysterious lady; her presence was bone chilling."
"Did you get to catch her face?" asked Elijah.
"Every woman wore a mask for the masquerade,
But I heard death and ceremony,
Before I stopped listening.
Had to walk away before anyone caught on to me.
I grabbed you to let you know,
You have to save your homie. Like Poe in some real trouble."
"I mean, he did say he made a mistake?"
"Naw, his mistake was going to that place.
Since last night, I've been feeling some type of way."
Elijah asked,

Why Did You?

"Why did you set up that man?
He's not a stranger, why did you set him up in his plans?
I thought when you were younger, you wanted to be a leader.

In front of me, I see a follower, not being his own man.
Why Did You?"
Aiyden picked up his mask and tied it around his face,
Before walking away.
Elijah wanted to run to the ceremony and warn his homie.
"Hey, bruh, check on my mom."
Those words echoed through Elijah's head.
Now remembering the last thing Poe said,
He had to find Mrs. Nia, now running deeper down the alley…

***

She looks so beautiful picking up her clothes.
Look at him, just laid out on the floor, Aminah thought.
"Come on, babe, I just want a little more."
"After this ceremony, you can have it anytime for sure.
I need you to get ready," Aminah was saying before walking out the door.
Lying on the floor, he started to remember.
His Mistake
In the silence, he was breathing as one.

Fingers over his lips, done in private.
She went left, she went right, why did she have to be so submissive?
I should have thought on these consequences,
How I was feeling, her warm hands made me feel better.
Now I'm thinking I should have gotten out all together.
The lines I crossed can break a union forever.
I keep apologizing for my weakness to pleasure.
He keeps thinking that he should have never made **His Mistake.**

***

Aminah was looking in the mirror, noticing the smile on her face.
The dress lay on her skin in just the right way.
Her hair, she had to fix.
Listening in the distance, she heard the voices of those two twins talking shit.
Looking around, she went into the last stall,
Sitting on the toilet, raising her feet.
"Rose, last night, now tell me," said Muna.
Aminah thought, *Rose?*
Luna started kicking the stall door open,
Making Kung Fu noises.

"Rose, tell me," said Muna.
Luna kicked another door open.
"Luna, not another door," said Rose.
"Rose, please, I want to know what it was like, please," Muna said.
What happened last night? thought Aminah.
"I think I saw Poe when he was on drink number three.
He was vibing to the party.
Standing there looking sexy,
Something I knew I couldn't have.
And I know he knew my face.
Then I thought, *we are in a masquerade*.
Putting on that mask, I had some tight lingerie.
When I saw he wanted to leave,
I grabbed his hand, lured him into an empty space.
I couldn't waste time, I wanted to be
<u>The Best He Ever Had.</u>
I knew what his girl wouldn't give.
He didn't have to tell, I had my fingers over his lips.
Anything he wanted to do was my gift.
This was my fun, my power.
I stood up first, over him, I towered.
Had him feeling dumb.
The smile on my face, was from the chain events that would become,

And before everything was done, I wanted to be
The Best He Ever Had.
"I wanted to give him some bachelor booty," said Rose.
As her hips were moving, Luna asked, "Did you call your best friend?"
Rose said, "Yeah, in the morning. I wanted to tell her
that her man satisfied her best friend when she was horny.
And I love him from the crown on his head,
To wiggly toes on his feet," snickered Rose.
The girls started giggling.
Then they heard an undeniable scream…

***

(14 Years Ago)
"These will be the last tears I cry.
I would rather die than let those tears fall."
Looking upon Jodi and Kathleen,
The crowd started screaming,
"Jodi and Kathleen, our future king and queen.
Jodi and Kathleen have been chosen for royalty."
He couldn't wake from his dream.
As he heard those ceremony bells clanging,
His ears started ringing.

***

(Present Day)
"Sir Mycki left the king, but I can't find the boy," said Ravana.
"It's almost time, the king is mine.
I want those ceremony bells clanging for me this time."
Azel grabbed his weapon, towards the king, he started stepping.
"Jodi knew this day would come.
He knows where this hatred comes from.
In his death, there will be honor, because it will come from
My Hands.
My hands will deliver a fatal blow.
For me to be king, all the land must know,
I was the one to deliver the fatal blow.
It will be done by
My Hands.
As Azel got closer to the king,
His back turned, because to the crowd he was speaking.
He started to hear a faint thing,
Then it turned into an undeniable scream.

Again, as an older man, he felt as if he was in a dream.
Underneath his feet, the ground started shaking.
And before the ceremony began,
The ceremonial bells started clanging,
Leaving his ears yet again ringing…

***

"People of Judeawai, this will be the second official ceremony announcing our future king and queen.
I would like to remind the tribe, this ceremony celebrates our peace.
It shows our unity for our community," said Jodi.
"Poe and Aminah, you will see shortly.
This ceremony will begin in less than 15 minutes, please find your seats."
Kathleen gazed upon her king,
Watching the tribe, listening to him as he spoke.
Just as King Denali did before, at their ceremony.
The crowd chanted.

<u>King and Queen</u>

"Our future king and queen.
What will our generation see?
Jodi and Kathleen,
Our future king and queen,

Have been chosen for royalty.
We were honored, we were loved,
As their
King and Queen
As Kathleen came back to reality,
She started realizing
Azel getting closer to her king.
The way he was approaching, didn't seem right.
Her heart dropped in her stomach, when she knew
Azel was coming for his life.
Where's Mycki? Someone needs to protect our king.
As she tried to move, the ground started shaking,
Dropping the queen to her knees.
Hands over ears, she heard an undeniable scream.

***

So many faces have come out today,
To celebrate. I have to go back to my place.
The old folk were sipping on wine.
Children were running past.
Couples in the streets, kissing.
Since I woke up, I've been having a bad feeling.
Last night, I knew, was a bad decision.
My parents told me to stay home, why didn't I listen?

Orion was the only one hitting.
Those twins, Luna and Muna, are so unforgetting.
Making love, in the living room,
Muna doing the splits.
"Why do I keep getting into shit?"
"Hey, kid."
Looking around in the crowd, he just swore he thought he heard his name.
"Hey, kid."
Someone must be calling for their child.
This celebration was getting more wild.
I have a feeling it's time to get away now.
As he was walking, someone grabbed his neck, dragging him into the alley,
Slamming his face on the wall.

Aiyden

What a traitor, telling the enemy what we plan to do.
Your mask was off, I saw you make that move.
I've been nothing but a homie to you.
I have a knife, for a permanent mark, to show the truth.
Do you hear what I'm saying?

Aiyden

"Grab his arms and don't let go."
"Orion, what are you doing?"

"I've been having you followed and I don't like the way you've been moving,
Always assuming, you never even asked me why I'm doing what I'm doing."
"Then, why?"
"Royal blood is pure and should not be mixed with their kind.
All things are necessary.
Even if I have to, I'll take a life,
To protect what's right.
We will live in the dark,
No longer needing light."
"What you are saying is lies."
Orion looked upon Aiyden,
Telling the ones he was with to rip his shirt.
Pressing the knife on Aiyden's skin,
In a line straight down,
With another line across, on the top.
"T! Orion, what are you doing to me?"
Aiyden was holding his tears, this pain made it hard.
The tears flowed when he saw the letter "R".
Orion was pressing harder with the letter "A".
The knife pressed harder in the middle of his chest.
That's right, the letter "I".
As Orion was pressing down, the knife went straight to stomach.

When Orion dropped to his knees,
He was in too much pain to recognize that scream…

***

Shaking on the toilet, what she just heard, she couldn't believe it.
Her fingers were over her man's lips,
Giving him her body and she called that a gift.
Oh, Grandmother, this happened last night.
Her hands caressed his face,
Fingers gliding to waist.
And because he was my man, this was her only opportunity.
No time, she could waste.
Rose!!!
<u>How Could You Do This</u>
How, after cutting ties,
You still want to play on my line,
Calling my phone in the morning,
Seeing how I was doing.
Complimenting on my great grandmother's dress.
How I was feeling, I confessed.
What the hell you mean, his best?
Rose!!! My best friend.
<u>How Could You Do This</u>

"Aminah, I need you to calm down."
Aminah thought, *she kept calling my phone, mocking my dress.*
The same one my great grandmother stitched.
"Aminah, I need you to breathe."
Aminah started rocking back and forth, praying.
"Adir, I need you here.
Help me see clear."
Grabbing her hair, rocking, she didn't recognize what was going on.
"Aminah, you're getting too angry, I have to leave your body."
Hands over her eyes, tears were coming. Trying not to cry.
She got to experience what's mine
Them kissing, making love, biting fingers.
Her, doing magical stuff, flashed before Aminah's eyes.
"I want Rose to die!!!"
"Aminah, please, calm your mind, please, I'm trying to leave."
Just then, Aminah looked left, and she saw something she couldn't believe.

It's A Dream

What I saw, had to be a dream
When I looked left, I saw an angel trying to get out of me.

Out of my left shoulder blade, was growing a wing.
My left eye started to change. I could actually see.
I felt the pulling and tugging.
The angel being was talking to me,
The only thing that makes sense.

It's A Dream

"Aminah, listen to me."
Aminah quieted her thoughts for a second to listen.
Her voice sounded familiar.
"Yes, I am an angelic being living inside you,
And your emotions are colliding with my spirit.
What I'm feeling, I fear it."
On the left side of Aminah's body, she was feeling power,
Surging through muscle and veins, the angel felt divine pain.
Anger was rising, at an alarming rate.
"Aminah!!! Calm your emotions.
To get out of you, I have to find a faster way."
"I wanted to give him some bachelor booty."
Aminah thought, *what did that female just say?*
One of the twins asked, "Did she call her best friend?"
"Her man satisfied her best friend when she was horny,
And I love him from the crown on his head,

To the wiggly toes on his feet."
What she just heard, Aminah couldn't believe
Her best friend mocked her love,
She couldn't believe as she was thinking about
Poe's wiggly feet.
Crying, sitting on a toilet, hiding behind a stall,
While these girls were giggling.
"Aminah, please—"
Before the angel could finish,
A sound came out of Aminah's mouth,
A scream, to knock those girls to their knees.
So much hatred made the ground start shaking.
In her head, harmony was playing.
Hatred started singing.

The Song Has Just Been Sung

Purge this world in fire.
Expose to the village, who is the liar.
This song has just been sung.
Consequences on what he's done.
Purge this world in fire.
Expose to the village who is the liar.

The Song Has Just Been Sung

8. A Forgotten Dream

(Baby Crying)

She hasn't gotten used to waking up this early in the morning.

Outside, the birds were singing, some of the town folk were talking.

(Baby still crying)

"Oh, Peace, you must be hungry."

She made her way to the kitchen,

Already knowing what she was about to start fixing.

Pancakes, eggs, you could hear the bacon sizzling.

(Baby still crying)

"Oh, Peace, I'm coming."

As breakfast was finished,

The ground started shaking.

Dishes shattering on the floor.

He was walking out the door.

Fed up, don't want to hear any more.

Loud sounds hitting the ground,

she couldn't hear Peace now.

Heat was rising, the upstairs was burning.

"Peace!!!"

There were screams outside,

Squeals you wouldn't want to hear.

Telling her feet to get her baby,

Skipping steps, looking out the window, to an image she knew
She would never forget, fire falling from skies.
Hearing the townsfolk's cries.
It's time to move now.
Fire clinging to the walls, there was a path to her son's room.
This fire was taking lives.
The heat was rising from outside.
In Poe's room, she went.
Looking in the crib, where did her son go?
Did he take Poe out the door?
Running and jumping steps,
Those flames are making her sweat.
Outside, hands were coming out of dirt.
Death was coming.
Fire was falling.
The skies were calling.
She screamed for her baby, "PEACE!!!"
Looking around, where can he be?
Heads sprouting like flowers,
The dead clinging to life.
What a sight.
Above, she saw a light,
An angel of some type.
Looking up, she asked for
Help

My son, can you help find?
Protect us in these troubling times.
I want what's mine,
My Peace!!!
Light above, please, can you?
Help
Above, flapping wings, the angel stayed,
Pointing a light towards her best friend Erykah's place.
The light left in a different way.
Sky is red, clouds are black.
The fire is back.
She started running, around corners turning.
Her feet stopped when she saw someone burning.
This town, this culture, the fire was destroying.
On a pole, roped down, a lady was burning.
She smelt the melting of flesh.
With a note on top, "HER FAULT".
The flames were too hot to get close.
No one in sight, fire falling,
There was no one to help to save a life.
She heard crying.
"My baby."
What she saw was devastating.
She had to find her baby.
Feet weren't moving,
Stayed looking at the lady.

Burning, no one to save her.
Her beautiful city was glowing.
It seemed as if the heat wanted to speak.
There was a girl running in the shadows.
There was something that was familiar.
About the shifty little figure.
HER BABY!!! Now, feet are moving,
In a direction that's unknown.
Where was her baby?
The skies were crying.
"Peace, I'm trying."
The screams were getting closer.
"NIA!"
"The clouds are talking."
Her eyes opened to a baby crying,
While Mother Kawana was holding Peace.

Mother Kawana

A mother of the village,
Watchful over her children.
Whether you came from her or not, did not make the difference.
When you cried, she listened.
If you had parents, or didn't.
To have her in your life, was a blessing.
Respect to

Mother Kawana

"Baby, I saw you resting and sleeping.

Seemed as if you were dreaming.
I walked to Poe's room, and in his crib, I saw him playing.
When he saw me, he was smiling.
Started to throw toys, he was wilding.
Well, anyway, I picked him up and started walking around.
We passed your room, he was still giggling and smiling.
Went to the kitchen, came back upstairs.
Poe started crying as if he could sense something I couldn't.
I tried to soothe him, but he wanted me in here."
"That's weird. I was having a nightmare," said Nia.
"I mean, there were fire and people."
"Hush it now, child. It was just a dream, forgotten if you ask me.
I believe nightmares are imagery our eyes don't want us to see.
Yet the brain is as wild and free and can seem as reckless as can be.
The nightmare is in the mind.
Sometimes your brain can leave clues in chaotic signs."
"Mother Kawana, there was fire,
Burning people alive.
The dead clinging to life.

The punishment was their fault.
Girls running in shadows.
I saw an angel."
"I heard if you dream of an angel, that usually means it's life or death," stated Mother Kawana.
"Erykah! There was a light pointing at her house. Can I go check on her, to make sure everything is all right?"
"All you do for me to help out, baby, I would watch Poe all night.
Plus, he's a good baby with a lot of energy," said Mother Kawana.
Nia started to get ready to go to her friend's house, Thanking Mother Kawana for all she did.
"Be safe, the moon is out," replied Mother Kawana…

***

"Boy, can you please stop with all that crying? You know what's a part of life?"
"What?"
"Dying, and I want you to know, I'm very proud of the grandson you've become.
Sure, you could be a nicer husband, a better father. But you have a second chance with your newborn daughter.

She's irresistible and a treasure."
Outside, the rain started pouring.
The skies were snoring.
Mud was forming.
"She would be a lotus, something special, my little me."
"Baby, you are going to have to let her be free.
Listen to your wife, I do believe she would lead you right.
Remember this…"
"Remember what? Granny, remember what? Erykah!!! She's not waking up."
In this dark room, his granny started to shine.
Her whole being was bright.
He'd never seen such a light.
Trying to cover his eyes,
Couldn't believe he was seeing an angel, out of his granny rise.
The light glowed.
Interest in the baby, it showed.
The brighter it got, the figure itself was becoming more transparent.
"You have to be a better parent."
He was imagining the light, disappearing in his baby.
Words were being spoken.
Let Her

Let her be wild and free.
Let her roam the world, but protect by all means.
Let her be a light to shine.
Let her be innocent.
This is a second chance.
Let her be your daughter.
Let Her
He just heard his granny speaking.
"Erykah!!!" the man started screaming.
"Erykah, it's about Aminah."
Erykah, meeting him outside,
looked in her husband's eyes and asked, "Why is he crying?"
The rain couldn't take his tears.
There was pain and joy in those eyes.
He said, "My grandmother just died."
Holding her man in the rain, trying to soak in as much pain,
Shielding him from lightning,
Trying to kiss away the hurt.
"Get away from me, my granny was the only thing living who loved me.
Get away from me; you don't love me."
Trying to embrace him back,
She accidentally tore his shirt.
His favorite shirt, stitched by his grandmother.
"I'm leaving!!!"

The thunder snatched his words, his voice.
Walking away was his choice.
She went to go get her daughter.
There was a light shining from Aminah
Looking around she couldn't see the grandmother.
Wondering why he had to leave her.
Walking into their home.
Trying to keep Aminah warm.
"Why am I not enough!"
Erykah thinking to herself what is that girl yelling about?
Placing Aminah in her crib.
Questioning what she did.
This is not fair.
Sitting downstairs, in her favorite chair,
Not knowing how to feel,
There was knocking on the door.
The vibration, she could feel.
"Erykah, open the door, it's me, Nia."
She stared at the door a bit
Before she opened it.
"Girl, I have to tell you about this crazy dream.
It had to do with fire.
Little girls who look like your daughter.
There was this angel.
Mama Kawana said that it meant life or death.
In the dream, the light pointed here.

Walking up, I could have sworn, screams, I could hear."
"Nia, my husband's grandmother just died," Erykah said.
"Listen, my dream, it had to do with death and life. Girl, with this baby, you should be very proud. With your husband, love you can finally allow."
"Nia! Shh, such things you shouldn't say aloud. The oldest is upstairs," Erykah said.
"Nia!!!"
Erykah shook her head, saying, "She has been in her room all
day screaming, about nothing,
she don't even know
Her great-grandmother just died."

***

"Another celebration, another year."
"King Denali, are you saying something?" asked the one who was his right.
He has once or twice saved the king's life.
"I want to shake a whole society.
What do the people want, what's the word?"
"We need to give leadership opportunities to the ones of no royal blood."
"Why would I do that?"

"It would show unity in our very own community."
"Yes, and we will call it a ceremony.
Boy, lucky seven, we will celebrate every year,
Which celebrates our peace, to be grateful we're not living how we used to be."
"So, we will have a ceremony, for what?"
"This Ceremony
Will unite our community.
Change minds on what is royalty.
Giving a chance to a non-royal.
In this ceremony, I will announce our next king and queen.
King Denali will make history,
Because of
This Ceremony."
"Do you know what that would do? Why?"
"Well, it's something a king can do, but you are right.
For something like that, I would need a sign,
To let me know I'm not going out of my mind."
King Denali was looking out into the night skies.
"I want the people to know I tried something great in my lifetime,
For this beautiful melanated, pretty city.
Where the people are witty, from sunup to sundown.
It's so busy…"

His Sign
What could that be in the night sky?
A light with a different shine,
For what he wanted to do for his city.
It was his time.
History will write his name.
They will say he followed his heart.
The angels provided.
His Sign
"In seven years, I will announce our future king and queen.
For my city, I will give a grand ceremony,
Unifying our community."
It was always something soothing,
When the rain was pouring.

9. A Dream Come True

"Nia!!! This is all your fault."
Opening her eyes, feeling pain from wrist,
Leaking from stomach, last thing she remembered was someone calling her name.
Why was she in so much pain?
"Where's my Peace?"
Not able to see her face, she heard, "He's not coming."
Laughter echoed.
Nia saw a figure in the shadows…

***

"Baby, you make me feel all brand new.
All I love is you.
This belief holds so true."
Singing, lying on the floor,
Poe heard a woman's screams through his door,
Piercing his ears, in a fetal position.
"POE!!! The city will know of your lies."
That was Aminah's voice, but very angry.
Looking for his clothes, then putting his pants on.
"I have to get to Aminah."
Things were falling, pictures getting knocked off walls.
He had to leave the room.

Opening the door, he turned right.
While running, his wrist started to be in pain.
"Peace!!! Now he was hearing his mother calling his name.
Making another right,
Running into someone who had a knife.
There was evil in those eyes.
He smiled and said, "Poe, I'm here to take your life."
He swung and Poe ducked.
Trying to move to the left.
On Poe's foot, Ravana stepped.
There was nowhere for Poe to go.
Poe thought quickly, then hit Ravana in the nose.
The contact intensified the pain in Poe's wrist.
"Peace!!!" He just heard his mom scream.
I'm coming, Thinking this, while feeling a strong impact on his teeth.
Another hit in his eye, Poe couldn't see.

Your Life is Mine

"I'm going to kick in every rib.
When I kick like this, you won't breathe.
Future king? You going to bow to me.
I will smash this vase upon your face.
Give in, there is no reason to try.

Your Life is Mine

Poe grabbed for Ravana's leg,

Feeling a boot to his face instead.
His own blood, he drank.
Powerful kicks to the ribs,
Made more ribs crack.
"I told you, your life is mine," Ravana was saying while he grabbed his knife.
No longer able to move with the searing pain in his back,
"PEACE!!!" before all went black, he heard his mother scream.

***

Zig-zagging through people, the townsfolk were pushing.
The ground was shaking, a piercing scream,
As if it was out of dream.
He had to find Mrs. Nia by any means.
"Where could she be? Shouldn't she be close by,
To her son's ceremony?"
Deeper into the city, Elijah went.
He ran by a courtyard that seemed to be empty.
On a second glance, he saw, roped to a pole, a lady.
Running closer, he got to see,
Couldn't believe what his eyes were receiving.

Breathing stopped, his feet were locked to the ground.
She stayed hanging there, not making a sound.
Whom he had been looking for, was now found.
In front of him, he saw his homie's mom,
Bleeding out.
Dropping to his knees, crying,
Who Has Done This?
Who has taken the mother of our future king?
To hang a woman to a stake
and claim this is her mistake.
Who has taken from our Peace?
She was a mother to me.
Who has taken from my family?
Who Has Done This?
Nia opened her eyes, seeing Elijah crying.
Out of her mouth, words were trying.
"Peace!!!" in her mind, she was screaming.

***

Shit, he's really bleeding, Orion thought.
Ground shaking, people crying, ladies screaming.
Talking to the ones he was with, he said, "Grab him."
Twist and turns, down alleyways.
"What is going on?" questioned Orion.

Aiyden could barely stand, dealing with this unbearable pain.
Orion knew they had to find a way out,
Before they get caught with this bloody body.
Twisting and turning.
"Great, an empty courtyard."
Running faster, he noticed an opportunity as he was getting closer.
Elijah was crying on his knees next to a roped up, dead lady.
Blood, he was covered in.
"Leave Aiyden to me and go tackle that man. And when you do, put this knife in his hand."
Leaving Aiyden, for Orion to carry.
"The choice you make, better be right, cuz believe it or not,
I'm trying to save your life," Orion whispered to Aiyden.
Out of nowhere, Orion started screaming, "It was that man, get him. I saw it!!!"
As people were running, certain folks started noticing.
Hearing a desperate call for help,
A crowd formed, looking at the blood on the boy.
"It was him. He hung her and stabbed my friend."
The crowd asked Aiyden who stabbed him.

With the little strength he had left, Aiyden was pointing at Elijah.

Elijah tried to speak, but Orion kicked him in his teeth.

"Why would we want to listen to somebody
Who has disturbed our Peace for centuries?
And you took this lady's life and tried to take the life of a friend of mine." Mustering tears in his eyes, he cried.

Some tribe members, decided the young man must be taken alive for his crimes.

Someone screamed, "Hang him like he hanged her."

A lady screamed, "Stab him like he did him."

They all chanted,

"He Gets What He Deserves

Whatever the punishment, you deserve it.

To rot in a cell, you deserve it.

The pain you took from someone's child.

How could you take life from a woman in our tribe?

Whatever we decide,

To burn him alive.

Don't let his sins confuse your conscience.

The lesson will be learned because

He Gets What He Deserves."

Furious, the crowd was getting,

Shouting and spitting.
Vile, this young man must be.
Nia's still there bleeding, screaming in silence.
The crowd yelled, "This destruction was caused by his violence."
One said, "Rope him up, cut him open and watch him die today."
"Or," one said, "you can make him a slave, where he is punished day after day."
A man knelt down for Elijah to see,
With a smile of greed, and said,
<u>**"You'll Be A Slave To Me,**</u>
Punished for your crimes in this society.
A slave, you'll be interrupting centuries of peace.
Forget who you used to be.
You are now a slave to me.
Your new life revolves around me.
At night, you will pray for a grave.
Every day, you will be in pain.
<u>**You'll Be A Slave To Me."**</u>
Elijah's wrist were being tied.
His brain couldn't register that Aiyden lied.
But why?
"I didn't do it!!!" Elijah cried.
Kicking Elijah again, Orion said, "Enough, with these lies."
Elijah, they continued to tie.

"This is because of your crimes," the crowd chanted.
A woman walking by looked and said,
"We don't care if you cry; they should do worse, the way you took that lady's life."
Elijah's mind was racing. "This isn't right, how did I take Mrs. Nia's life?"
Dragging him away, a fight Elijah tried.
Tears in his eyes, looking at Mrs. Nia one last time,
He saw her lips moving.
She heard her son was coming.
They covered his mouth, before he could let anyone know she was still alive…

***

"Poe!!! The city will know of your lies.
Purge in this fire!!!"
The ceiling crumbled in a stall.
Rose and the twins couldn't believe Aminah was rising.
Surprisingly looking different, half human, half something,
There was a wing flapping to one side.
"Rose, you wanted this forbidden fruit.
Because of your fiery, passionate time,

This village will suffer from fire falling from the skies.
The dead will come alive."
Rose thought this was not her friend flying in the skies.
"That can't be Aminah. She heard everything I did to her dude."
The twins, next to Rose, were looking confused.
No longer giggling, eyes fearful.
Blue skies changing red.
"Poe!!! This is for your crimes!!!" Aminah said.
White clouds becoming black,
Those skies opened, fire rained.
As the fire was falling, Rose heard her village in pain.
Screaming, clinging to life were all the same.
Aminah was the only being uncontrollably laughing.
The twins heard the village dying.
Being strong in each other's arms, they were trying.
Ground shaking, buildings breaking,
Rose knew she had taken it too far this time.
How could she save her life?
Fire was falling in the broken ceiling.
The smoke and fire were making it hard to see things.

Rose grabbed the twins, saying, "We gotta get out."
The flames was following those three,
As if, like an angel wanted it to be,
Aminah looked down on these treacherous times.
The fire was the seed to birth the dead alive.
"Poe!!! This is because of your lies."

***

The platform was waving; there was screaming in the air,
Really piercing to the ear.
The king knew he had to get everybody out of there.
Looking for Mycki, he saw something shining.
With Azel covering his ears, realization kicked in, and anger set in.
"Azel, you were going to slay me, before the platform started shaking."
With fire in his eyes, he looked upon the king and said,

"These Hands
Will deliver the fatal blow.
On this ceremony, you'll die before everyone you know.
The king will be slain.

Your queen will have deep pain.
She'll be consoled by
<u>These Hands.</u>"
Anger fumed in the king's heart after what Azel had just said.
"You talk on my queen," said the king.
Azel smiled, grabbing his weapon. "Indeed."
Azel knew straight up, he couldn't kill the king.
Jodi knew in his heart he was going to kill Azel on this ceremonious day.
The final challenge had to come this way.
"Poe!!! This is for your crimes."
Azel and Jodi both stopped, looking toward the skies.
The ground was shaking, the platform was breaking,
Crumbling, trapping the king.
Azel saw this as an opportunity.
His hands were going to end the king.
Azel had to stop when he heard a different type of agony.
Looking around, he saw folks running, people on fire.
Flames falling, why on this day were the skies calling?
Destruction was everywhere.
Destiny was his, taken by fate.

Fire started raining in this very place.

***

What a scream, to knock even the queen to her knees.
So much fear, the image of his face played in her head.
"Beware of the fire from the skies," was what the old man had said.
Kathleen was frozen, as stone.
She watched as the children cried.
Families trying to survive.
Now focused, she needed to get her king.
Mycki was gone; something must be wrong.
Any challenge given to her man, she knew he could stand.
She needed to get Jodi, to help finish Azel.
As she watched, her husband fell,
Stumbled as the platform crumbled.
The queen knew Azel would strike.
He would be king if he took his life.
Flames started raining inside,
The heat immediately started to rise,
Separating Azel and Jodi for a short time.
Realizing her husband was stuck, nowhere to escape,

More flames came to consume lives,
The king couldn't break free.
This fire in front of them was burning her man alive.
Villagers tried.
The king cried, pain and agony in his voice.
Desperate, he was trying to survive.
More flames, set the platform ablaze.
"Poe!!! You lied
These villagers will suffer because of your crimes.
My flames will take many lives.
Giving souls to the dead to be alive.
The wounds of the earth has not healed.
All will come to understand how I feel."
Some villagers couldn't believe they watched the death of their king.
Some said, "We have to protect the queen."
Kathleen couldn't breathe, what did she just see?
She couldn't move.
Over her husband, the fire was dancing,
Being natural, playing.
The queen wanted to see the king hop out the flames.
She was waiting.
Crying, she said,

"Come Back To Me
Pinch me, please, wake me from this dream.

When I open my eyes, we will be preparing for this ceremony.
The old man said, 'Beware of the fire, from the skies.
On this day, that flame will claim many lives.'
Jodi, my king, come back to me.
Why did the flames have to take that life?
A husband from a wife?
My heart won't beat right, please,
<u>Come Back To Me."</u>
Some of the village ladies grabbed their queen.
"We have to get out of here."
Now there were many screams,
Not just from the skies.
It was now, the ones who burned,
Tried to still cling to their own lives.
The queen looked upon one of the ladies and asked, "Where's Mycki?"

***

Before Ravana could turn around,
He was being knocked to the ground with brute force.
He looked in the direction from where it came.
Dusting himself off, he said, "Of course, Mycki."
"You will not lay another hand on our future king."

Poe lay lifeless next to Ravana's feet.
Ravana, reaching for his weapon, said, "We'll see."
He didn't see Mycki move, it was with controlled speed.
Mycki, tripping his feet, connecting fist to jaw.
Hitting him strong, Ravana was going through a wall.
Mycki was sweating, realizing fire was falling.
Placing Poe on his shoulders,
He knew he had to run.
Hitting Ravana that hard, he knew the challenge he'd just begun.
Running down hallways, he knew both of them had to get out of that place.
Every single minute counted, he knew he couldn't waste.
He knew he had Poe.
Somehow, he would have to connect with the king.
So many townsfolk were outside,
Watching the fire consuming so many lives,
Hoping the fire wouldn't fall on them this time.
And as quickly as it had come, the fire from the skies ceased.
It was a moment of silence.
Then out of the ground, heads started to spring.
This place, he knew he had to leave,
But not without the king and queen.

Looking for a safe area for the lifeless body of Poe to be,
He knew his number #1 obligation was for his king.
Finding a shelter for safety,
He knew he had to start a fire,
To bring warmth to this lifeless body.
Outside, he heard the innocent cry.
Tears came to his eyes when he thought on those lives.
He thought to himself, *I need to find who altered these peaceful times.*
How did we fall into this?

Destruction

Destruction can come at any point and time.
The peace in this city can't be repaired.
My father said, 'Life will not be fair.'
Centuries worth of peace, this can't end here.
I swear on this night, I will help fix this mess by my king's side.
Destruction will not take my life .
Somehow, we'll find a way to make things right.
I will not give in to this.

Destruction

Mycki couldn't believe all this was real.
Looking at the young man lying still,
He knew Ravana was there to kill.

This must have been Azel's will.
Knowing all this,
to the ceremony, he must go back,
To protect King Jodi.
The safety home started warming.
Placing Poe in the corner of the shadows of safety,
Before leaving him, he started saying,
"You're Safe.
Future king, if you can hear me, please wait.
When I get to the king and queen, I will bring them back to this place.
I promise we will get the man who hurt you this way.
Future king, I hope you can hear.
When you wake, have no fear.
Just know,
You're Safe."

***

Calling for their children,
Everyone is running.
Chaotic all around,
Heads of the dead, sprouting out of the ground.
Laughter, you can hear up ahead,
Someone enjoying the destruction instead.
Dancing dips in despair,

Moving hips to the fair in life.
Excited to even witness this sight,
At peace with himself, he was
Realizing finally,
<u>He Was Not Out His Mind</u>.
They said I was crazy most of my life.
I was the one who predicted the fire from the skies.
What I said, they thought were lies.
I told so many people countless times.
The children laughed when I walked by.
The queen herself thought
<u>He Was Out His Mind.</u>
As an ordinary old man, they thought it was I.
This is such a night, death is gripping life.
Trying with all its might.
The whole time, I was right.
Hearing the misery,
Was really hurting.
He had nobody to recognize that he was sane.
In all this disarray, he shouted to the heavens for his brain.
Those dreams and visions were all the same.
Fire fell from the skies.
The voice spoke on the lies.
What king will come in due time?

***

Running down the halls,
The flames hugged her arm.
Dancing, loving her strong,
Picking up speed, wishing this intolerable pain gone.
Her appetite was weak.
Why did she eat
<u>The Forbidden Fruit?</u>
That taste, oh, so sweet.
The passionate juice dripped out my mouth.
There were tingles in my feet.
I held on for just a moment.
My lust had a hunger to devour.
I poured like the Nile.
The sensation left me with a devilish smile.
I'm burning now.
Why did I eat
<u>The Forbidden Fruit?</u>
"Help, our friend is on fire," the twins screamed.
The flames burned half her face; that was something the twins couldn't believe.
Of help, they were in dire need.
"Help!" screamed the twins down the hallways.
Just as they turned the corner, the flames went away.
"My face!" screamed Rose.

The skies replied, "This is your punishment, I suppose."
"Help!!!" the girls screamed,
Getting the attention of the queen.
Katheen knew the girl in the middle was in pain indeed.
It was the way she screamed.
Burning flesh, she smelled,
Reminding her of when the king fell.
Her eyes swelled with smoke.
Out of this building, she knew they must go.
Kathleen asked Muna what was her friend's name?
Muna said, "I don't know."
Again, the queen started asking her ladies, "Where is Mycki?"
The right hand to the king,
Someone she knew who could protect the queen.
Such a structure was falling.
"The dead are alive," Judeawai was calling.
She kept seeing Jodi's face,
Asking herself,

Why, on This Ceremonious Day,

Must we see hurt and pain?
Bury loved ones in the grave?
Our king had to be taken today.
I can't erase his face.
Seeing the dead come alive in this way,

We got our Peace snatched away.
Why, on This Ceremonious Day?
One of the ladies asked the queen which way.
Kathleen started to remember some of the things
Jodi would say and said, "I know of a safe place."

***

Nia, where could she be? Erykah was thinking.
Before the ceremony, they were supposed to meet.
Together, they would sit.
Everything was going right, this was such a
wonderful time.
Aminah's family members were walking by,
Smiles on faces, saying, "You must be very
proud."
Looking out in the crowd,
She didn't notice the crazy old man approaching
who accidently knocked her to the ground.
She saw children chasing him down,
Chanting behind,
"Beware of the fire from the skies.
The flames will take many lives."
Looking back, the old man said, "Get out now!!!"
Before he dipped around the corner.
Trying to get up, mad that nobody warned her,
Not seeing Nia really concerned her.

She saw her earlier, talking to Aminah.
"Erykah, why are you not inside? I heard the king announce the ceremony will begin in the next 15 minutes," said Tris, also looking around as she asked,
"Have you seen Nia? We begin shortly. I need the parents of both parties."
Tris made her way to the king, to see to his last minute needs.
The building, this ceremony for her daughter, was so breathtaking.
As a baby, she would have never imagined such a celebration.
The crowd was shouting.
The drums were banging.
Horns was singing.
Erykah thought she was honestly dreaming.
Then pain came to her brain,
With an undeniable, familiar type of screaming.
Worried now, Erykah knew she had to look for her baby.
As she pushed through the crowd, the earth started shaking,
Everyone running in all different directions.
She looked up in the skies,
As her daughter lifted on high,
With one wing flapping to one side.

There was a different look in her baby's eyes.
She saw hurt and pain.
"Poe!!! The city will know of your lies.
Purge in this fire!!!"
Debris from the building started falling.
Her eyes stayed on her daughter as she thought,
<u>What Happened To Her?</u>
She's half-human and whatever.
What happened to our treasure,
The baby to make her parents better?
Who crossed my baby?
Where was her glow?
"Rose, you wanted this forbidden fruit."
Where were Aminah's petals?
My husband promised she would be special.
How did we not notice,
There was a corruption in our lotus.
I need answers.
<u>What Happened To Her?</u>
"This village will suffer from fire falling in the skies.
The dead will come alive.
Poe, this is for your crimes."
Listening to what her daughter just said, she didn't know how to react.
The skies turned red and the clouds were black.
Then the flames hit the ground.

Those squeals came loud.
Everyone started running around,
Trying to avoid the fire.
Unlucky ones were burning.
Erykah knew she had to start moving
and avoid the fire raining from the skies.
"Poe!!! You lied.
These villagers will suffer because of your crimes.
My flames will take many lives,
Giving souls to the dead to be alive.
The wounds of the earth have not healed.
All will come to understand how I feel."
The fire opened the soil.
Heads starting sprouting.
Erykah couldn't believe Nia's dream would be real.
Running, avoiding the heat and flame,
With her own eyes, she saw a
Corpse body changing.
Morphing, looking human.
We all looked the same.
A crowd was dispersing.
She had to follow to see where they were going.
Are they going somewhere safe?
What she saw broke her in a different way.
Why did Nia's dream have to be so true?
Nia, roped to a stake.
Mother Kawana was standing in front of her.

The only thing she heard was, "I'm sorry for my son."
Above her head, was a sign saying it was her mistake.
Nia finally tried to speak, her blood dripped, she was very weak.
"Nia, how can this be?" Erykah asked.
Nia finally said, "This destruction is your seed."
Erykah screamed, "Your son lied, this is because of his crimes."
So enraged, Erykah struck Nia,
Saying, "I will end your child.
He will suffer for his crimes now."
She struck her so hard, Nia hit the ground in the courtyard.
So much anger made her pierce Nia's heart.
Nia thought,

I Will Protect

I will protect my son at all costs.
Even when you thought I lost,
From the grave, I will protect.
Adir, do you hear?
My son,

I Will Protect.

Erykah struck her friend's rib cage.
Nia's soul went away.
Mother Kawana looked at Erykah.

Erykah said, "I heard you say this is your son's fault.
Nia's son altered my daughter."
Mother Kawana said, "She dreamt this 21 years ago."
Erykah said, "I have a place we can go…

***

She marveled in the destruction.
Those girls followed her instruction.
In the shadows, she bowed down and said,
"Our Vow.
On this day, our vow changed a whole society.
On this day, I dealt with the hatred towards that lady.
On this day, I proved my loyalty to the shadows.
On this day, I've embraced
Our Vow."

10. A Failed Challenge

"Kathleen!!!" was the last thing he heard from Jodi The No Name,
Before he was engulfed in those flames.

(15 Years Ago)
"I spoke to you leaders six years ago,
 about my opportunity to change our community,
Announcing our next king and queen at this ceremony."
On this particular day, the rain was pouring.
You could hear the impact of the rain drops outside.
"I have a solution of who will take this crown, it will conclude in a fight,
Royal vs none.
Azel vs Jodi.
There was chatter amongst the leaders in the society.
"My king, the crown has always been royal," said the father of Azel.

Axel
A savage, a man, an heir
A leader, a father, at the table, he had a chair.
Royal, proud, heritage, it was in his blood.
His family was next in line.
It was predicted in time.

He prepared his son to shine.
No challenge in their family,
will they fail.
That was what his father taught.

Axel

King Denali, in fury, asked,
"Do you question the signs from above?
They gave us a light,
An opportunity to share lineage with our community."
The other leaders looked at Axel with anger in their eyes.
One said, "Your seat on the throne, can be next in line
If your son can win the challenge.
We can't stand behind a king who can't win challenges."
Axel pondered on everything that had just been said.
The faces around were clear, yet his background was becoming red.
The king stepped closer to Axel and asked,
"Does your family accept the challenge,
I mean, does your son accept this challenge?"
Axel stared in his king's eyes and said,
"Yes, we, I mean, yes, he will accept this challenge."

The king smiled and said,
"Great, non-royal vs royal.
Jodi vs Azel.
Let the challenge begin."

***

(Present)
"POE!!! YOU LIED.
Azel wondered what was going on.
MY FLAMES WILL TAKE MANY LIVES.
He started to look for the voice in the sky.
Scanning around the room, he watched his queen cry,
Screaming for No Name to come back to her.
Thinking quickly on his feet, he knew he needed to find Ravana.
This ceremonious building was on fire.
Never in a million years, would he thought he would see
fire falling from the skies.
The city of Judeawai had a cry.
He watched as the dirt hugged the dead, clinging for their lives.
Azel couldn't believe all that was going on outside.
Running faster, knowing Ravana he had to find.
Turning the corner at the perfect time,

Azel saw so much anger in Ravana's eyes, ,
"*He's Going To Die.*"
He's going to die, because I failed.
Breaking his bones will make him cry, he will feel he is in hell.
He is going to wanna die, after he had to interfere.
This challenge will show his fear.
He will see the hate in my eyes.
It will be evident, it will be clear.
"*He's Going To Die.*"
Azel told Ravana the king was dead,
Not by his hands but by the flames instead.
Ravana heard everything Azel said.
Looking worried, he said, "The boy is not dead."

***

(15 Years Ago)
"As your king, I nominate Jodi to represent the non-royal side."
The rain poured harder outside.
On torches, fire was inside.
A glare could be seen in everyone's eyes.
The king and his right hand, Alo, were preparing this time.
In his stomach, Azel could feel the butterflies.
All these years, it was his time.

His father looked at him and said,
"Please Astonish Me.
Show the leaders it will be you who leads.
The crown will stay with the royal seed.
Your mother and I are proud we birthed an heir-to-be.
Connect to your ancestors, they will give strength.
Son, since birth, I knew the heavens blessed thee.
It's time to let the common seed know you have to be birthed royalty.
For your father, I ask you to
Please Astonish Me."
"As the father of the next heir, I nominate Azel to represent the royal blood, to keep tradition alive."
After Axel said those words, the room grew quiet.
One could only hear the fire's crackle.
At this point, the king's words got violent.
His tone could slice silence.
"The challenge will be a dual amongst the two.
Thus, who wins in this challenge will be the next king.
If Azel wins, that would mean I bore false witness upon my sign towards the
Royal family. If you win, there would be no opportunity for the common seed to achieve royalty ever again. That's only if he wins."
Azel knew what this time meant,

All those hours on training spent.
In his heart, he knew he had to win.
He could feel the heat of the flame.
Never, would he give the crown to Jodi The No Name.
He has no lineage to claim.
This will not be

A Failed Challenge.

I swung for his face.
He ducked. I didn't guard my face.
My knee hit his chest plate, I felt the pain and ache.
It lay perfect under his shirt.
His fist connected to my jaw, my head hit the wall.
No, not like this, I will not fall.
The Royal seed is depending on me.
He swung, I dodged with speed,
Hitting him in his temple with ease,
Dropping Jodi to his knees.
I know stars are the only thing he sees.
Knocking him with all his might,
I'm going to give them a fight.
I looked towards my father,
unable to see his strike.
Searing pain, I felt.
Dragging me to the fire, he said my face he was going to melt.

I reached for his belt, I twisted him in a way
He fell to the ground.
The pain was intense, but I felt I had some time now.
I felt a kick, blood I spit.
Again, dragging me to the flames.
I can't lose to No Name.
Tripping his feet, Azel knew he wasn't expecting
Slashing his calf as he was falling.
In the air, he flipped. I felt a kick,
more blood I spit.
My head hit the ground. I heard a ringing sound.
More dragging, more tripping, flipping, kicking, spitting.
The king taught No Name that was his advantage.
I can't believe this turned out to be

A Failed Challenge.

"Jodi, our next to be," the king acknowledged.
His royalty training was about to begin.
The king announced,
"Jodi's seven-year training will begin. When he is finished, he will take the throne.
Alo, write this down as law.
For those who feel they shall deserve a second chance,
For you to be king,
You need to take his life with your own hands.

When a King Announced is next,
He will be protected for seven years, to claim the crown.
If the king dies of a natural disaster,
The King Announced will be protected for the duration of his time.
Unless one takes his life with their own hands,
The throne will be open for those chosen to rule.
Until the King Announced's training is complete.
If, in seven years, the King Announced does not claim his seat,
the one ruling can stay his term.
This law is written
And can't be changed until the time is met.
Signed, King Denali
And since we're in a time of peace, there's no need for killing.
Azel, you fought well and you also will have a seat amongst the leaders, after you tend to your wounds."
Leaders laughed as they left.
My father left.
So alone, I felt.

***

(Present)

Ahh.
He felt as if someone just cut a lifeline.
So much pain throughout his body.
"Mommy." Where was his mother, he thought.
Ahh,
Trying to breathe, grabbing his side.
Where am I? Poe thought.
Someone tried to kill me.
He looked around at what seemed to be an empty space,
Gripping his waist, trying to get on his feet,
Falling on his face.
What the hell was going on? This can't be from his wrongs.
His chucks were scuffed, blood on his feet.
It was hard for him to see,
you can't think when you can't breathe.
Ahh,
He was tasting death,
trying to catch his breath.
Yet can't, there's no air in hell.
There's no need for earthly possessions in here.
"Peace!!!"
Please hear.

I Will Protect You
I will protect my Peace On Earth
I'm behind any mistake.

I will prove you're heaven sent.
Wipe the tears off your face.
Your purpose is to heal the hurt.
I will take you to different heights.
This place is not safe.
Get out if you want your life.
My beloved,
I Will Protect You.
"I'm near."
Getting up was easier, at least he could stay on his feet.
Out of one eye, he could see.
Trying to find a second to think.
Was this because of the king?
He remembered hearing Aminah's scream.
Did he see the future in his dream?
First, he needed to save his life.
Whoever left him, kept him in the corner,
With a fire.
It felt impossible to move.
One step at a time was all he could do.
In his head, another voice he heard saying,
'Training Lesson #1
As King Announced, you need to believe
Anything that faces you,
don't run, conquer.

Learn, in any obstacle, as king, it's possible to achieve.
You need to take the word can't,
Hold the cross(t) to your chest,
and believe you can.

Training Lesson #1
He needed to escape, ignoring the pain in his face.
As he walked past a mirror, he didn't recognize himself in his own reflection.
Anger helped ease the pain.
Coming to self, focused on present.
He heard the screams from the outside,
About a fiery rain.
He took three deep breaths before saying,

"I Am Peace On Earth.
Say your name loud,
So the stars can twinkle
And the sun will smile.
A protection will come over now.
Peace is a train on thought.
Remember what you've been taught.
The heart knows.

I Am Peace On Earth
Finding his mother, was now a priority.
He knew she would be able to tend to his injuries.
Probably have an answer to what was going on.

He froze when he heard some footsteps approaching.

***

Azel looked at Ravana and asked,
"Are you sure it's this place?"
Ravana, still angry, said, "I saw Mycki go this way, and knowing Mycki, this would be it. By how it's tucked away, he would think this would be safe."
They both knew this boy couldn't stay alive.
Azel asked, "What about Mycki?"
Ravana replied, "I'll take his life."
Walking in on what appeared to be an empty shelter,
Ravana thought it was a little too quiet.
Both moving, silent,
prepared for any violence.
They looking around.
Poe knew he could not move.
Ravana said, "I know he's in here."
Azel felt it too,
This was his last chance to the throne,
An opportunity he couldn't lose…

***

"Jodi!!! Why did you leave me?" screamed the queen.
Listening to the queen, rocking her friend,
Rose couldn't believe the day had turned this way.
This morning, she was beautiful, now she was burnt in the face.
Luna was thinking, *how did the plan go wrong?*
Quite frankly, she didn't know what was going on.
Muna was sitting alone, not knowing what to say,
Watching the queen break down.
"My king!!! Come back to me," cried Kathleen.
Luna was rocking her friend Rose,
Pondering on such events.
Did Aminah command fire?
Was she really a half angel in the sky?
Did we cause this, when she heard our lies?
Her feelings was supposed to be hurt,
A marriage even broken, but
This Was Not Supposed To Happen.
I was looking forward to change,
Just wanted to see hurt and pain.
I've disrupted what three generations have never seen.
The beauty was young.
Before destruction, we sang a song.
A heart was going to get hurt.

Why did the plan work
So well,
We brought hell. She had a plan,
Yet sins sprouted from the grave.
In our plan,
This Was Not Supposed To Happen.
Just last night, I was having the time of my life,
Luna thought.
The lingerie made my body look nice.
By the middle of the party,
Everything was all right.
The champagne had me, like
Feeling myself, ready for a promise
That was given by
The Lady In The Shadows.
She spoke, yet this lady you could not see.
There was an evil in her speech.
Disgusted by Peace.
Made such a plan which was going to disrupt The Ceremony.
The orders were given by
The Lady In The Shadows.
I was watching the party
and she snuck up behind me.
The dark silhouette showed she also was in lingerie.

She said, "The average never deserved the power, they would easily fall into desires, in a heart would spark a fire.
It's so much better loving on Royals.
The king will feel the Royal's pain.
Have fun tonight, do things your way."
She was so close behind, I could feel her,
Without touching her.
"Look at him, chilling, having a good time. What drink is he on?"
Luna looking at Poe having a good time, watching all the women pass by.
She knew, he knew Aminah was in for the night.
Turning her head to the side,
Never looking behind,
Saying, "My sister just gave him his third."
Luna could feel the excitement rising behind her.
She heard the mystery lady say,
"It's time to go get her,"
Before disappearing in the shadows.
Luna knew at this point there was no going back.
"MY FACE!!!" Luna snapped to reality with Rose on her lap.
The queen kept asking the heavens to bring her husband back.
"Muna." Muna looked at her twin sister,
Rocking her best friend

Who was in so much pain.
You could just see it in her face.
"What?" she said.
Luna asked, "What are we going to do?"
Muna knew they had to move,
Rose needed help.
Then, there was her sister.
Just looking around, she could see destruction everywhere.
Under the queen, was most likely the way they would find care.
"We'll stay here," Muna replied to her sister.
One of the queen's ladies was trying to ask her which way.
Looking around, she couldn't recognize her Judeawai.
Tribe folk were screaming, "The dead are living."
"Queen Kathleen!" they thought they heard.
Which way should they go?
They saw a man running up the road.
"Queen Kathleen!" His voice was a bit clearer.
The queen looked up, saying, "Mycki?"

***

"Are we going to save him?"
Orion thought of the question being asked.

He knew his once friend's condition was really bad.
Orion also heard a voice in the shadows saying, "Come follow me if you want to help your friend Aiyden."
He was screaming in agony.
When they went in the shadows, he heard her say, "You thought quickly on your feet when you blamed him."

***

Ravana's voice gave Poe chills.
He was the one who just tried to kill him.
Hearing the other voice saying,
"I need the crown,"
As they were moving things around.
Poe knew they were getting closer now.
Lifting his head, saying, "To The Man sitting on high, I need your protection here."
In the blink of his eyes, there was a bright light.
The entire room grew white.
Levitating in front of him, was King Jodi.
None of this seemed right.
Jodi was floating, staring Poe down.
He began by saying,
"I Am You Now.

The crown is now declared yours.
Nature's wrath took my life for sure.
I will teach you what a king fights for.
The value, the honor of being Non-Royal.
It's a cycle, my body is feeding the soil.
I will try to keep you alive,
To claim your crown.
There's no need to worry.
I Am You Now.**"**
Poe felt a surge of energy.
In a blink of an eye, the white was gone.
He was back in reality.
Poe was now listening.
Jodi told him, "Pick up that metal rod next to your feet."
It felt like the perfect weapon.
"When I get a hold of him, I'm breaking all his bones."
Azel said, "I don't care how you do it,
I just need the throne.
The Royal blood in leadership is coming back home."
Hurting, Poe tried to get in a fighting stance, yet stepping too soon,
There was a squeaky sound in the floor.
He counted to four.
One, two, three, four.

He heard footsteps racing to his room.

***

"When I get a hold of him, I'm breaking all his bones," said Ravana.
"I don't care how you do it. I just need the throne."
Right then, he heard a squeaky sound in the floor.
Placing the index finger over his lips,
Pointing in the direction,
Both of them started running.
Azel knew this moment would change his life.
Bursting through the door,
He saw his #2 get struck with a lightning strike.
Looking at Azel, he heard Poe say,
"Come on if you want to take my life."
Azel looked at Poe and smiled,
Knowing fighting him would be compared to whooping a child.
He would not dare go through
<u>Another Failed Challenge.</u>
He pointed a pipe. I dodged the strike.
Hitting his face with all my might,
The boy fell on the floor.
More kicks to the face, kicks in his rib.
Ravana got up and went straight for the kid.
Poe grabbed for the metal pipe.

Ravana felt another strike.
When Poe wasn't looking, I cut him on his right cheek with my knife.
Not paying attention, he felt a surge of electricity,
Pain all over.
With that weapon, he struck my shoulder,
Kicking me over.
When he was grabbing me,
I saw the fury of Jodi.
The face of No Name was all I could see.
He grabbed my head, pounding it on the floor.
I was hearing a familiar ringing sound.
Dragging my face in the dirt,
Hitting me with his weapon until it hurt.
His strike was trying to take my life.
Ravana hit Poe across his face with something,
Distracting him for a minute.
We need to get out.
The king was fighting in Poe's body,
That was his advantage.
I can't believe this turned out to be
<u>Another Failed Challenge.</u>

Author Note

I pray you enjoyed the story of Poe. Just as much as I enjoyed writing it. Years in the making, understanding the characters. What story did I want to tell? This was different from my other poetry books. I wanted to push my writing in the art of poesy. When I was younger, I liked reading about the Hero's tale. As a writer I wanted to write a tale myself from the beginning to the end. Things I have experienced in life, stories I've read have inspired this novella.

Such as the idea of Dante's Inferno with love, hell, and mythology. The Count of Monte Cristo inspired the betrayal. Other works which have inspired me are Dragon Ball Z (R.I.P Akira Toriyama) and Star Wars.

Thank you, Royal Media for being patient in this process and Marla Willams-VanHoy for editing this work. I appreciate the family, friends and fans who continue to encourage me to write. This is just the beginning story of Poe. I look forward to writing more in this world. Thank you Gad Elite Book Covers for a dope cover.

Epilogue

T.R.P. Series
By: Brooks "Poetry" Crittenton

It was joy to his ears as he heard
The cries and the moans.
His crew set fire to all the town's homes,
Raiding in houses & palaces.
Our action is malice.
We are The Last Pirates,
Living in violence,
Dwelling in private,
Conquering town after town.
Our fear comes in silence.
We come to take,
Every time our life is on the line.
Who wants it more?
When faced in the eyes of death, who will cleave to life?
Are you ready for that type of fight?
"Pirates, this city is ours," she said.
The crew chanted, loud chants,
Drinking to their hearts' content.
"The City of Gold will be next," her sword was raised in the air,

They all heard her declare.
In her captain's eyes, she stared,
The only time he would get stuck with a glance.
His treasure, whom he shares pleasure and his joy over the fiery waters.
Skin of dark hue, she knows how to soothe.
"Filthy Pirates, you will feel my pain also."
A man saying this right before he let his last hope loose.
She was his only target, oh, how she stood on high.
Declaring their prize,
The captain saw his love fall before his eyes.
So many times, they conquered together, loved one another.
"Who has decided to take a piece of me?"
Running towards his lady,
The crew started going crazy.
An iron rod went through her organs.
"City of Gold…" she was still urging.
Love was speaking blood,
A language he never understood.
Many of his victims spoke in blood,
Trying to come up with their last words.
They usually only come out slurred.
More blood words she was speaking.
The captain was frustrated because he was not understanding.

What was love saying? he was thinking.
Not like this; he had to be dreaming.
His crew started screaming,
"Captain, we found the cause and meaning.
This man took your love's last breath."
Laying his last sense of humanity on the ground,
Around, they could hear the fiery, crackling sound.
The man looked the captain in his eyes
And said, "You will feel my pain too. You took what was mine."
The captain recognized an emblem.
He was an representative for The City of Gold.
Calmly, the captain said, "You will suffer for what you have taken.
Your curse will be you survived.
Tonight, will play in your mind.
Wishing you died, trust me, you will live in grief.
I will keep you alive."
His crew heard their captain roar,
"Take what you want. To The City of Gold, we go!!!"
This town took his lady.
They acquired riches.
He lost his reason.
Any cling to humanity, he was leaving.
Tonight, he saw his love bleeding.
She was conquering, then died.

The world will know of The Real Pirates this time.

Purchase at http://www.payhip.com/tlkpoetry

Other Books by This Author

www.ingramcontent.com/pod-product-compliance
Lightning Source LLC
Chambersburg PA
CBHW071215160426
43196CB00012B/2307